book
life

A BOOK LOVER'S JOURNAL

COMPILED BY WILLIAM MCKAY

A division of Quarto Publishing Group USA Inc.
276 Fifth Avenue, Suite 206
New York, New York 10001

ROCK POINT and the distinctive Rock Point logo are trademarks of
Quarto Publishing Group USA Inc.

© 2014 by Rock Point

ISBN-13: 978-1-93799-458-7

Printed in China

2 4 6 8 10 9 7 5 3 1

www.rockpointpub.com

TABLE OF CONTENTS

"A BOOK, TOO, CAN BE A STAR, A LIVING FIRE *to* LIGHTEN *the* DARKNESS, LEADING OUT *into the* EXPANDING UNIVERSE."

—*Madeleine L'Engle*

"A reader lives a thousand lives before he dies. . . . The man who never reads lives only one." George R. R. Martin's words might stand as the motto of millions of men and women for whom books are essential daily companions. Whether fiction or nonfiction, the little paper objects that Stephen King called "uniquely portable magic" inhabit our lives with their stories, but also with their mysteries. Finding out what's next or what's behind the curtain becomes its own reward. As the author's partner in crime, we keep our night-light burning, always leading us to a conclusion that beckons us on to the next book. Thus reading becomes a lifetime journey through space and time, a voyage that renews us even as it reminds us we are not alone.

Franz Kafka described books as the axes, or icebreakers, for the frozen seas within us. What then is a reader's journal? Perhaps if clearly seen and attentively kept, it is an explorer's log to discoveries and ports of call along the way, pointers to finding ourselves amidst blizzards of information.

"TO LEARN TO READ IS TO LIGHT A FIRE; EVERY SYLLABLE THAT IS SPELLED OUT *is a* SPARK."

—*Victor Hugo*

READING WISH LIST

"So many books, so little time." Frank Zappa was right. Our ever-expanding mental list of what we want to read always makes us second-guess our own choices of what we do read. Wise readers have no compunctions about following the practice of bookseller's son Samuel Johnson, who once responded to a friend's inquiry with a tart, "No, sir, do you read books *through*?"

However you deal with it, your lifetime reading wish list beckons. Do you want to finally immerse yourself in sprawling Russian epics or catch up on Dickens or the thirty-eight Discworld novels you might have missed? Or perhaps you would love to carve out time for the three volumes of Shelby Foote's Civil War histories that have been gathering dust on your shelves ever since you discovered them at the secondhand book sale.

Your personal wish list might be on any topic, genre, period, or author. (Who among us hasn't yearned to read every book by a favorite author?) *What matters is that even though we know we can't read everything we want in our multimillion book world, we keep reaching and reading and gathering in the goodies . . .*

READING WISH LIST

Date: _____

Title: _____

Author: _____

Where I heard about it: _____

_____

Why I want to read it: _____

_____

_____

~~~~~~~~~~~~~~~~~~~~~~~~~~~~~~~~~~~~~~

Date: _____

Title: _____

Author: _____

Where I heard about it: _____

_____

Why I want to read it: _____

_____

_____

Date: _____

Title: _____

Author: _____

Where I heard about it: _____

_____

Why I want to read it: _____

_____

_____

~~~~~~~~~~~~~~~~~~~~~~~~~~~~~~~~~~~~~

Date: _____

Title: _____

Author: _____

Where I heard about it: _____

_____

Why I want to read it: _____

_____

_____

READING WISH LIST

Date: _____

Title: _____

Author: _____

Where I heard about it: _____

_____

Why I want to read it: _____

_____

_____

~~~~~~~~~~~~~~~~~~~~~~~~~~~~~~~~~~~~

Date: _____

Title: _____

Author: _____

Where I heard about it: _____

_____

Why I want to read it: _____

_____

_____

Date: _____

Title: _____

Author: _____

Where I heard about it: _____

_____

Why I want to read it: _____

_____

_____

~~~~~~~~~~~~~~~~~~~~~~~~~~~~~~~~~~

Date: _____

Title: _____

Author: _____

Where I heard about it: _____

_____

Why I want to read it: _____

_____

_____

READING WISH LIST

Date: _____

Title: _____

Author: _____

Where I heard about it: _____

_____

Why I want to read it: _____

_____

_____

~~~~~~

Date: _____

Title: _____

Author: _____

Where I heard about it: _____

_____

Why I want to read it: _____

_____

_____

Date: _____

Title: _____

Author: _____

Where I heard about it: _____

_____

Why I want to read it: _____

_____

_____

~~~~~~

Date: _____

Title: _____

Author: _____

Where I heard about it: _____

_____

Why I want to read it: _____

_____

_____

READING WISH LIST

Date: _____

Title: _____

Author: _____

Where I heard about it: _____

_____

Why I want to read it: _____

_____

_____

~~~~~~~~~~~~~~~~~~~~~~~~~~~~~

Date: _____

Title: _____

Author: _____

Where I heard about it: _____

_____

Why I want to read it: _____

_____

_____

Date: _____

Title: _____

Author: _____

Where I heard about it: _____

_____

Why I want to read it: _____

_____

_____

~~~~~~

Date: _____

Title: _____

Author: _____

Where I heard about it: _____

_____

Why I want to read it: _____

_____

_____

READING WISH LIST

Date: _____

Title: _____

Author: _____

Where I heard about it: _____

_____

Why I want to read it: _____

_____

_____

〜〜〜〜〜〜〜〜〜〜〜〜〜〜〜〜〜

Date: _____

Title: _____

Author: _____

Where I heard about it: _____

_____

Why I want to read it: _____

_____

_____

Date: _____

Title: _____

Author: _____

Where I heard about it: _____

_____

Why I want to read it: _____

_____

_____

〰〰〰〰〰〰〰〰〰〰〰〰〰〰

Date: _____

Title: _____

Author: _____

Where I heard about it: _____

_____

Why I want to read it: _____

_____

_____

READING WISH LIST

Date: _____

Title: _____

Author: _____

Where I heard about it: _____

_____

Why I want to read it: _____

_____

_____

~~~~~~

Date: _____

Title: _____

Author: _____

Where I heard about it: _____

_____

Why I want to read it: _____

_____

_____

Date: _____

Title: _____

Author: _____

Where I heard about it: _____

_____

Why I want to read it: _____

_____

_____

~~~~~~~~~~~~~~~~~~~~~~~~~~~~~~~~

Date: _____

Title: _____

Author: _____

Where I heard about it: _____

_____

Why I want to read it: _____

_____

_____

READING WISH LIST

Date: _____

Title: _____

Author: _____

Where I heard about it: _____

_____

Why I want to read it: _____

_____

_____

~~~~~~~~~~~~~~~~~~~~~~~~~~~~~~~~~

Date: _____

Title: _____

Author: _____

Where I heard about it: _____

_____

Why I want to read it: _____

_____

_____

Date: _____

Title:_____

Author: _____

Where I heard about it:_____

_____

Why I want to read it: _____

_____

_____

~~~~~~~~~~~~~~~~~~~~~~~~~~~~~

Date: _____

Title:_____

Author: _____

Where I heard about it:_____

_____

Why I want to read it: _____

_____

_____

"I CANNOT REMEMBER THE BOOKS I'VE READ ANY MORE THAN *the* MEALS I'VE EATEN; EVEN SO, *they* HAVE MADE ME."

—*Ralph Waldo Emerson*

MY BOOK LOG

According to a 2014 Pew Research Center survey, a typical American reads five books a year. The number of books you read most likely surpasses that number, but even if the lesser tally is accurate, it still amounts to dozens and dozens of books perused over a lifetime. Over time, however, memories of those books, even of their titles, dissolve as we move forward.

In an incandescent passage, Ursula K. Le Guin wrote, "The unread story is not a story; it is little black marks on wood pulp. The reader, reading it, makes it live: a live thing, a story." A book log keeps the stories alive with your own notes, thoughts, and quotes. Attentively kept, it becomes a diary of the mind, a record of the things that keep us going.

MY BOOK LOG

Date: _____ Overall Grade: **A** **B** **C** **D** **F**

Title: _____

Author: _____

My thoughts about this book: _____

_____

_____

_____

_____

_____

_____

_____

_____

Memorable ideas or quotes: _____

_____

_____

_____

_____

RATE THIS BOOK:

Ease of reading: A B C D F

Memorable characters: A B C D F

Originality: A B C D F

Quality of writing: A B C D F

Read other books by this author? Y or N

Would you read it again? Y or N

MY BOOK LOG

Date: _____ Overall Grade: **A B C D F**

Title: _____

Author: _____

My thoughts about this book: _____

_____

_____

_____

_____

_____

_____

_____

Memorable ideas or quotes: _____

_____

_____

_____

_____

_____

_____

_____

_____

_____

_____

_____

_____

RATE THIS BOOK:

Ease of reading:		A B C D F
Memorable characters:		A B C D F
Originality:		A B C D F
Quality of writing:		A B C D F

Read other books by this author?   Y or N

Would you read it again?   Y or N

MY BOOK LOG

Date: _____ Overall Grade: **A B C D F**

Title: _____

Author: _____

My thoughts about this book: _____

_____

_____

_____

_____

_____

_____

_____

Memorable ideas or quotes: _____

_____

_____

_____

_____

_____

_____

_____

_____

_____

_____

_____

_____

RATE THIS BOOK:

Ease of reading: A   B   C   D   F

Memorable characters: A   B   C   D   F

Originality: A   B   C   D   F

Quality of writing: A   B   C   D   F

Read other books by this author?   Y or N

Would you read it again?   Y or N

MY BOOK LOG

Date: _____ Overall Grade: **A B C D F**

Title: _____

Author: _____

My thoughts about this book: _____

_____

_____

_____

_____

_____

_____

_____

_____

Memorable ideas or quotes: _____

_____

_____

_____

_____

_____

_____

_____

_____

_____

_____

_____

_____

RATE THIS BOOK:

Ease of reading:	A	B	C	D	F
Memorable characters:	A	B	C	D	F
Originality:	A	B	C	D	F
Quality of writing:	A	B	C	D	F

Read other books by this author?   Y or N

Would you read it again?   Y or N

MY BOOK LOG

Date: _____ Overall Grade: **A** **B** **C** **D** **F**

Title: _____

Author: _____

My thoughts about this book: _____

_____

_____

_____

_____

_____

_____

_____

_____

Memorable ideas or quotes: _____

_____

_____

_____

_____

_____

_____

_____

_____

_____

_____

_____

_____

RATE THIS BOOK:

Ease of reading: A   B   C   D   F

Memorable characters: A   B   C   D   F

Originality: A   B   C   D   F

Quality of writing: A   B   C   D   F

Read other books by this author?   Y or N

Would you read it again?   Y or N

MY BOOK LOG

Date: _____ Overall Grade: **A   B   C   D   F**

Title: _____

Author: _____

My thoughts about this book: _____

_____

_____

_____

_____

_____

_____

_____

_____

Memorable ideas or quotes: _____

_____

_____

_____

_____

_____

_____

_____

_____

_____

_____

_____

_____

RATE THIS BOOK:

Ease of reading:	A B C D F
Memorable characters:	A B C D F
Originality:	A B C D F
Quality of writing:	A B C D F

Read other books by this author?   Y or N

Would you read it again?   Y or N

MY BOOK LOG

Date: _____ Overall Grade: **A B C D F**

Title: _____

Author: _____

My thoughts about this book: _____

_____

_____

_____

_____

_____

_____

_____

_____

Memorable ideas or quotes: _____

_____

_____

_____

_____

_____

_____

_____

_____

_____

_____

_____

_____

RATE THIS BOOK:

Ease of reading:	A B C D F
Memorable characters:	A B C D F
Originality:	A B C D F
Quality of writing:	A B C D F

Read other books by this author?   Y or **N**

Would you read it again?   Y or **N**

MY BOOK LOG

Date: _____ Overall Grade: **A** **B** **C** **D** **F**

Title: _____

Author: _____

My thoughts about this book: _____

_____

_____

_____

_____

_____

_____

_____

_____

Memorable ideas or quotes: _____

_____

_____

_____

_____

_____

_____

_____

_____

_____

_____

_____

_____

RATE THIS BOOK:

Ease of reading: A   B   C   D   F

Memorable characters: A   B   C   D   F

Originality: A   B   C   D   F

Quality of writing: A   B   C   D   F

Read other books by this author?   Y   or   N

Would you read it again?   Y   or   N

MY BOOK LOG

Date: _____ Overall Grade: **A   B   C   D   F**

Title: _____

Author: _____

My thoughts about this book: _____

_____

_____

_____

_____

_____

_____

_____

_____

Memorable ideas or quotes: _____

_____

_____

_____

_____

RATE THIS BOOK:

Ease of reading: **A B C D F**

Memorable characters: **A B C D F**

Originality: **A B C D F**

Quality of writing: **A B C D F**

Read other books by this author? **Y** or **N**

Would you read it again? **Y** or **N**

MY BOOK LOG

Date: _____ Overall Grade: **A   B   C   D   F**

Title: _____

Author: _____

My thoughts about this book: _____

_____

_____

_____

_____

_____

_____

_____

Memorable ideas or quotes: _____

_____

_____

_____

_____

_____

_____

_____

_____

_____

_____

_____

_____

RATE THIS BOOK:

Ease of reading: A   B   C   D   F

Memorable characters: A   B   C   D   F

Originality: A   B   C   D   F

Quality of writing: A   B   C   D   F

Read other books by this author?   Y or N

Would you read it again?   Y or N

MY BOOK LOG

Date: _____ Overall Grade: **A** **B** **C** **D** **F**

Title: _____

Author: _____

My thoughts about this book: _____

_____

_____

_____

_____

_____

_____

_____

_____

Memorable ideas or quotes: _____

_____

_____

_____

_____

_____

_____

_____

_____

_____

_____

_____

_____

RATE THIS BOOK:

Ease of reading:	**A** **B** **C** **D** **F**
Memorable characters:	**A** **B** **C** **D** **F**
Originality:	**A** **B** **C** **D** **F**
Quality of writing:	**A** **B** **C** **D** **F**

Read other books by this author?   **Y** or **N**

Would you read it again?   **Y** or **N**

MY BOOK LOG

Date: _____ Overall Grade: **A** **B** C D F

Title: _____

Author: _____

My thoughts about this book: _____

_____

_____

_____

_____

_____

_____

_____

_____

Memorable ideas or quotes: _____

_____

_____

_____

_____

_____

_____

_____

_____

_____

_____

_____

_____

RATE THIS BOOK:

Ease of reading: A B C D F

Memorable characters: A B C D F

Originality: A B C D F

Quality of writing: A B C D F

Read other books by this author?   Y or N

Would you read it again?   Y or N

MY BOOK LOG

Date: _____ Overall Grade: A   B   C   D   F

Title: _____

Author: _____

My thoughts about this book: _____

_____

_____

_____

_____

_____

_____

_____

_____

Memorable ideas or quotes: _____

_____

_____

_____

_____

RATE THIS BOOK:

Ease of reading: **A B C D F**

Memorable characters: **A B C D F**

Originality: **A B C D F**

Quality of writing: **A B C D F**

Read other books by this author? **Y** or **N**

Would you read it again? **Y** or **N**

MY BOOK LOG

Date: _____ Overall Grade: **A** **B** **C** **D** **F**

Title: _____

Author: _____

My thoughts about this book: _____

_____

_____

_____

_____

_____

_____

_____

_____

Memorable ideas or quotes: _____

_____

_____

_____

_____

_____

_____

_____

_____

_____

_____

_____

_____

RATE THIS BOOK:

Ease of reading:	**A B C D F**
Memorable characters:	**A B C D F**
Originality:	**A B C D F**
Quality of writing:	**A B C D F**

Read other books by this author?   **Y** or **N**

Would you read it again?   **Y** or **N**

Date: _____ Overall Grade: A   B   C   D   F

Title:_____

Author: _____

My thoughts about this book: _____

_____

_____

_____

_____

_____

_____

_____

_____

Memorable ideas or quotes: _____

_____

_____

_____

_____

RATE THIS BOOK:

Ease of reading: **A**   **B**   **C**   **D**   **F**

Memorable characters: **A**   **B**   **C**   **D**   **F**

Originality: **A**   **B**   **C**   **D**   **F**

Quality of writing: **A**   **B**   **C**   **D**   **F**

Read other books by this author?   **Y** or **N**

Would you read it again?   **Y** or **N**

MY BOOK LOG

Date: _____ Overall Grade: **A B C D F**

Title: _____

Author: _____

My thoughts about this book: _____

_____

_____

_____

_____

_____

_____

_____

_____

Memorable ideas or quotes: _____

_____

_____

_____

_____

_____

_____

_____

_____

_____

_____

_____

_____

RATE THIS BOOK:

Ease of reading:	A	B	C	D	F
Memorable characters:	A	B	C	D	F
Originality:	A	B	C	D	F
Quality of writing:	A	B	C	D	F

Read other books by this author?   Y or N

Would you read it again?   Y or N

MY BOOK LOG

Date: _____ Overall Grade: **A B C D F**

Title: _____

Author: _____

My thoughts about this book: _____

_____

_____

_____

_____

_____

_____

_____

_____

Memorable ideas or quotes: _____

_____

_____

_____

_____

_____

_____

_____

_____

_____

_____

_____

RATE THIS BOOK:

Ease of reading: A   B   C   D   F

Memorable characters: A   B   C   D   F

Originality: A   B   C   D   F

Quality of writing: A   B   C   D   F

Read other books by this author?   Y or N

Would you read it again?   Y or N

MY BOOK LOG

Date: _____ Overall Grade: **A** **B** **C** **D** **F**

Title: _____

Author: _____

My thoughts about this book: _____

_____

_____

_____

_____

_____

_____

_____

_____

Memorable ideas or quotes: _____

_____

_____

_____

_____

_____

_____

_____

_____

_____

_____

_____

_____

RATE THIS BOOK:

Ease of reading: A   B   C   D   F

Memorable characters: A   B   C   D   F

Originality: A   B   C   D   F

Quality of writing: A   B   C   D   F

Read other books by this author?   Y or N

Would you read it again?   Y or N

Date: _____ Overall Grade: **A**   **B**   **C**   **D**   **F**

Title: _____

Author: _____

My thoughts about this book: _____

_____

_____

_____

_____

_____

_____

_____

_____

Memorable ideas or quotes: _____

_____

_____

_____

_____

RATE THIS BOOK:

Ease of reading: A B C D F

Memorable characters: A B C D F

Originality: A B C D F

Quality of writing: A B C D F

Read other books by this author?   Y or N

Would you read it again?   Y or N

MY BOOK LOG

Date: _____ Overall Grade: **A B C D F**

Title: _____

Author: _____

My thoughts about this book: _____

_____

_____

_____

_____

_____

_____

_____

_____

Memorable ideas or quotes: _____

_____

_____

_____

_____

RATE THIS BOOK:

Ease of reading: A B C D F

Memorable characters: A B C D F

Originality: A B C D F

Quality of writing: A B C D F

Read other books by this author? Y or N

Would you read it again? Y or N

MY BOOK LOG

Date: _____ Overall Grade: **A** **B** **C** **D** **F**

Title: _____

Author: _____

My thoughts about this book: _____

_____

_____

_____

_____

_____

_____

_____

_____

Memorable ideas or quotes: _____

_____

_____

_____

_____

_____

_____

_____

_____

_____

_____

_____

_____

RATE THIS BOOK:

Ease of reading: A   B   C   D   F

Memorable characters: A   B   C   D   F

Originality: A   B   C   D   F

Quality of writing: A   B   C   D   F

Read other books by this author?   Y or N

Would you read it again?   Y or N

Date: _____   Overall Grade: **A   B   C   D   F**

Title: _____

Author: _____

My thoughts about this book: _____

_____

_____

_____

_____

_____

_____

_____

_____

Memorable ideas or quotes: _____

_____

_____

_____

_____

_____

_____

_____

_____

_____

_____

_____

_____

RATE THIS BOOK:

Ease of reading:	A B C D F
Memorable characters:	A B C D F
Originality:	A B C D F
Quality of writing:	A B C D F

Read other books by this author?   Y or N

Would you read it again?   Y or N

Date: _____ Overall Grade: **A   B   C   D   F**

Title: _____

Author: _____

My thoughts about this book: _____

_____

_____

_____

_____

_____

_____

_____

_____

Memorable ideas or quotes: _____

_____

_____

_____

_____

_____

_____

_____

_____

_____

_____

_____

_____

RATE THIS BOOK:

Ease of reading:	**A**	**B**	**C**	**D**	**F**
Memorable characters:	**A**	**B**	**C**	**D**	**F**
Originality:	**A**	**B**	**C**	**D**	**F**
Quality of writing:	**A**	**B**	**C**	**D**	**F**

Read other books by this author?   **Y** or **N**

Would you read it again?   **Y** or **N**

MY BOOK LOG

Date: _____ Overall Grade: **A** **B** **C** **D** **F**

Title: _____

Author: _____

My thoughts about this book: _____

_____

_____

_____

_____

_____

_____

_____

_____

Memorable ideas or quotes: _____

_____

_____

_____

_____

_____

_____

_____

_____

_____

_____

_____

_____

RATE THIS BOOK:

Ease of reading: A B C D F

Memorable characters: A B C D F

Originality: A B C D F

Quality of writing: A B C D F

Read other books by this author?   Y or N

Would you read it again?   Y or N

MY BOOK LOG

Date: _____ Overall Grade: **A   B   C   D   F**

Title:_____

Author: _____

My thoughts about this book: _____

_____

_____

_____

_____

_____

_____

_____

Memorable ideas or quotes: _____

_____

_____

_____

_____

RATE THIS BOOK:

Ease of reading: A   B   C   D   F

Memorable characters: A   B   C   D   F

Originality: A   B   C   D   F

Quality of writing: A   B   C   D   F

Read other books by this author?   Y or N

Would you read it again?   Y or N

MY BOOK LOG

Date: _____ Overall Grade: **A** **B** **C** **D** **F**

Title: _____

Author: _____

My thoughts about this book: _____

_____

_____

_____

_____

_____

_____

_____

_____

Memorable ideas or quotes: _____

_____

_____

_____

_____

_____

_____

_____

_____

_____

_____

_____

_____

RATE THIS BOOK:

Ease of reading: A   B   C   D   F

Memorable characters: A   B   C   D   F

Originality: A   B   C   D   F

Quality of writing: A   B   C   D   F

Read other books by this author?   Y or N

Would you read it again?   Y or N

Date: _____ Overall Grade: A B C D F

Title: _____

Author: _____

My thoughts about this book: _____

_____

_____

_____

_____

_____

_____

_____

Memorable ideas or quotes: _____

_____

_____

_____

_____

RATE THIS BOOK:

Ease of reading: A B C D F

Memorable characters: A B C D F

Originality: A B C D F

Quality of writing: A B C D F

Read other books by this author?   Y or N

Would you read it again?   Y or N

MY BOOK LOG

Date: _____ Overall Grade: **A   B   C   D   F**

Title: _____

Author: _____

My thoughts about this book: _____

_____

_____

_____

_____

_____

_____

_____

_____

Memorable ideas or quotes: _____

_____

_____

_____

_____

_____

_____

_____

_____

_____

_____

_____

_____

RATE THIS BOOK:

Ease of reading: A B C D F

Memorable characters: A B C D F

Originality: A B C D F

Quality of writing: A B C D F

Read other books by this author?   Y or N

Would you read it again?   Y or N

MY BOOK LOG

Date: _____ Overall Grade: **A B C D F**

Title: _____

Author: _____

My thoughts about this book: _____

_____

_____

_____

_____

_____

_____

_____

_____

Memorable ideas or quotes: _____

_____

_____

_____

_____

_____

_____

_____

_____

_____

_____

_____

_____

RATE THIS BOOK:

Ease of reading:	**A** **B** **C** **D** **F**
Memorable characters:	**A** **B** **C** **D** **F**
Originality:	**A** **B** **C** **D** **F**
Quality of writing:	**A** **B** **C** **D** **F**

Read other books by this author?   **Y** or **N**

Would you read it again?   **Y** or **N**

MY BOOK LOG

Date: _____ Overall Grade: **A B C D F**

Title: _____

Author: _____

My thoughts about this book: _____

_____

_____

_____

_____

_____

_____

_____

_____

Memorable ideas or quotes: _____

_____

_____

_____

_____

_____

_____

_____

_____

_____

_____

_____

_____

RATE THIS BOOK:

Ease of reading:	A B C D F
Memorable characters:	A B C D F
Originality:	A B C D F
Quality of writing:	A B C D F

Read other books by this author?   Y or N

Would you read it again?   Y or N

Date: _____ Overall Grade: **A** **B** **C** **D** **F**

Title: _____

Author: _____

My thoughts about this book: _____

_____

_____

_____

_____

_____

_____

_____

_____

Memorable ideas or quotes: _____

_____

_____

_____

_____

RATE THIS BOOK:

Ease of reading: A B C D F

Memorable characters: A B C D F

Originality: A B C D F

Quality of writing: A B C D F

Read other books by this author?   Y or N

Would you read it again?   Y or N

MY BOOK LOG

Date: _____ Overall Grade: **A B C D F**

Title: _____

Author: _____

My thoughts about this book: _____

_____

_____

_____

_____

_____

_____

_____

_____

Memorable ideas or quotes: _____

_____

_____

_____

_____

_____

_____

_____

_____

_____

_____

_____

_____

RATE THIS BOOK:

Ease of reading:	**A B C D F**	
Memorable characters:	**A B C D F**	
Originality:	**A B C D F**	
Quality of writing:	**A B C D F**	

Read other books by this author?   **Y** or **N**

Would you read it again?   **Y** or **N**

MY BOOK LOG

Date: _____ Overall Grade: **A   B   C   D   F**

Title: _____

Author: _____

My thoughts about this book: _____

_____

_____

_____

_____

_____

_____

_____

_____

Memorable ideas or quotes: _____

_____

_____

_____

_____

_____

_____

_____

_____

_____

_____

_____

_____

RATE THIS BOOK:

Ease of reading: A   B   C   D   F

Memorable characters: A   B   C   D   F

Originality: A   B   C   D   F

Quality of writing: A   B   C   D   F

Read other books by this author?   Y or N

Would you read it again?   Y or N

Date: _____ Overall Grade: **A** **B** **C** **D** **F**

Title: _____

Author: _____

My thoughts about this book: _____

_____

_____

_____

_____

_____

_____

_____

_____

Memorable ideas or quotes: _____

_____

_____

_____

_____

_____

_____

_____

_____

_____

_____

_____

_____

RATE THIS BOOK:

Ease of reading:	A	B	C	D	F
Memorable characters:	A	B	C	D	F
Originality:	A	B	C	D	F
Quality of writing:	A	B	C	D	F

Read other books by this author?   Y or N

Would you read it again?   Y or N

MY BOOK LOG

Date: _____ Overall Grade: **A B C D F**

Title: _____

Author: _____

My thoughts about this book: _____

_____

_____

_____

_____

_____

_____

_____

_____

Memorable ideas or quotes: _____

_____

_____

_____

_____

_____

_____

_____

_____

_____

_____

_____

_____

RATE THIS BOOK:

Ease of reading: A   B   C   D   F

Memorable characters: A   B   C   D   F

Originality: A   B   C   D   F

Quality of writing: A   B   C   D   F

Read other books by this author?   Y or N

Would you read it again?   Y or N

MY BOOK LOG

Date: _____   Overall Grade: **A   B   C   D   F**

Title: _____

Author: _____

My thoughts about this book: _____

_____

_____

_____

_____

_____

_____

_____

_____

Memorable ideas or quotes: _____

_____

_____

_____

_____

RATE THIS BOOK:

Ease of reading: **A B C D F**

Memorable characters: **A B C D F**

Originality: **A B C D F**

Quality of writing: **A B C D F**

Read other books by this author? **Y** or **N**

Would you read it again? **Y** or **N**

MY BOOK LOG

Date: _____ Overall Grade: **A B C D F**

Title: _____

Author: _____

My thoughts about this book: _____

_____

_____

_____

_____

_____

_____

_____

_____

Memorable ideas or quotes: _____

_____

_____

_____

_____

_____

_____

_____

_____

_____

_____

_____

RATE THIS BOOK:

Ease of reading:	A B C D F
Memorable characters:	A B C D F
Originality:	A B C D F
Quality of writing:	A B C D F

Read other books by this author?　　Y or N

Would you read it again?　　Y or N

MY BOOK LOG

Date: _____ Overall Grade: **A** **B** **C** **D** **F**

Title: _____

Author: _____

My thoughts about this book: _____

_____

_____

_____

_____

_____

_____

_____

_____

Memorable ideas or quotes: _____

_____

_____

_____

_____

_____

_____

_____

_____

_____

_____

_____

RATE THIS BOOK:

Ease of reading:	A B C D F	
Memorable characters:	A B C D F	
Originality:	A B C D F	
Quality of writing:	A B C D F	

Read other books by this author? Y or N

Would you read it again? Y or N

MY BOOK LOG

Date: _____ Overall Grade: **A B C D F**

Title: _____

Author: _____

My thoughts about this book: _____

_____

_____

_____

_____

_____

_____

_____

_____

Memorable ideas or quotes: _____

_____

_____

_____

_____

_____

_____

_____

_____

_____

_____

_____

_____

RATE THIS BOOK:

Ease of reading: A   B   C   D   F

Memorable characters: A   B   C   D   F

Originality: A   B   C   D   F

Quality of writing: A   B   C   D   F

Read other books by this author?   Y or N

Would you read it again?   Y or N

MY BOOK LOG

Date: _____ Overall Grade: **A   B   C   D   F**

Title: _____

Author: _____

My thoughts about this book: _____

_____

_____

_____

_____

_____

_____

_____

_____

Memorable ideas or quotes: _____

_____

_____

_____

_____

_____

_____

_____

_____

_____

_____

_____

_____

RATE THIS BOOK:

Ease of reading:	A B C D F
Memorable characters:	A B C D F
Originality:	A B C D F
Quality of writing:	A B C D F

Read other books by this author?   Y or N

Would you read it again?   Y or N

Date: _____ Overall Grade: **A** **B** **C** **D** **F**

Title: _____

Author: _____

My thoughts about this book: _____

_____

_____

_____

_____

_____

_____

_____

_____

Memorable ideas or quotes: _____

_____

_____

_____

_____

_____

_____

_____

_____

_____

_____

_____

RATE THIS BOOK:

Ease of reading: A   B   C   D   F

Memorable characters: A   B   C   D   F

Originality: A   B   C   D   F

Quality of writing: A   B   C   D   F

Read other books by this author?   Y or N

Would you read it again?   Y or N

MY BOOK LOG

Date: _____ Overall Grade: **A** **B** **C** **D** **F**

Title: _____

Author: _____

My thoughts about this book: _____

_____

_____

_____

_____

_____

_____

_____

Memorable ideas or quotes: _____

_____

_____

_____

_____

RATE THIS BOOK:

Ease of reading: **A B C D F**

Memorable characters: **A B C D F**

Originality: **A B C D F**

Quality of writing: **A B C D F**

Read other books by this author? **Y** or **N**

Would you read it again? **Y** or **N**

MY BOOK LOG

Date: _____ Overall Grade: **A** **B** **C** **D** **F**

Title: _____

Author: _____

My thoughts about this book: _____

_____

_____

_____

_____

_____

_____

_____

_____

Memorable ideas or quotes: _____

_____

_____

_____

_____

_____

_____

_____

_____

_____

_____

_____

RATE THIS BOOK:

Ease of reading:	A B C D F
Memorable characters:	A B C D F
Originality:	A B C D F
Quality of writing:	A B C D F

Read other books by this author?   Y or N

Would you read it again?   Y or N

Date: _____ Overall Grade: **A** **B** **C** **D** **F**

Title: _____

Author: _____

My thoughts about this book: _____

_____

_____

_____

_____

_____

_____

_____

Memorable ideas or quotes: _____

_____

_____

_____

_____

_____

_____

_____

_____

_____

_____

_____

_____

RATE THIS BOOK:

Ease of reading: A   B   C   D   F

Memorable characters: A   B   C   D   F

Originality: A   B   C   D   F

Quality of writing: A   B   C   D   F

Read other books by this author?   Y or N

Would you read it again?   Y or N

Date: _____ Overall Grade: **A   B   C   D   F**

Title: _____

Author: _____

My thoughts about this book: _____

_____

_____

_____

_____

_____

_____

_____

_____

Memorable ideas or quotes: _____

_____

_____

_____

_____

_____

_____

_____

_____

_____

_____

_____

_____

RATE THIS BOOK:

Ease of reading: A B C D F

Memorable characters: A B C D F

Originality: A B C D F

Quality of writing: A B C D F

Read other books by this author?   Y or N

Would you read it again?   Y or N

Date: _____ Overall Grade: **A B C D F**

Title: _____

Author: _____

My thoughts about this book: _____

_____

_____

_____

_____

_____

_____

_____

_____

Memorable ideas or quotes: _____

_____

_____

_____

_____

_____

_____

_____

_____

_____

_____

_____

_____

RATE THIS BOOK:

Ease of reading: **A   B   C   D   F**

Memorable characters: **A   B   C   D   F**

Originality: **A   B   C   D   F**

Quality of writing: **A   B   C   D   F**

Read other books by this author?   **Y** or **N**

Would you read it again?   **Y** or **N**

MY BOOK LOG

Date: _____ Overall Grade: **A   B   C   D   F**

Title: _____

Author: _____

My thoughts about this book: _____

_____

_____

_____

_____

_____

_____

_____

_____

Memorable ideas or quotes: _____

_____

_____

_____

_____

_____

_____

_____

_____

_____

_____

_____

_____

RATE THIS BOOK:

Ease of reading: A B C D F

Memorable characters: A B C D F

Originality: A B C D F

Quality of writing: A B C D F

Read other books by this author?   Y or N

Would you read it again?   Y or N

MY BOOK LOG

Date: _____ Overall Grade: **A   B   C   D   F**

Title:_____

Author: _____

My thoughts about this book: _____

_____

_____

_____

_____

_____

_____

_____

Memorable ideas or quotes: _____

_____

_____

_____

_____

_____

_____

_____

_____

_____

_____

_____

_____

RATE THIS BOOK:

Ease of reading: A B C D F

Memorable characters: A B C D F

Originality: A B C D F

Quality of writing: A B C D F

Read other books by this author? Y or N

Would you read it again? Y or N

MY BOOK LOG

Date: _____ Overall Grade: **A   B   C   D   F**

Title: _____

Author: _____

My thoughts about this book: _____

_____

_____

_____

_____

_____

_____

_____

_____

Memorable ideas or quotes: _____

_____

_____

_____

_____

_____

_____

_____

_____

_____

_____

_____

_____

RATE THIS BOOK:

Ease of reading: A   B   C   D   F

Memorable characters: A   B   C   D   F

Originality: A   B   C   D   F

Quality of writing: A   B   C   D   F

Read other books by this author?   Y or N

Would you read it again?   Y or N

MY BOOK LOG

Date: _____ Overall Grade: **A   B   C   D   F**

Title: _____

Author: _____

My thoughts about this book: _____

_____

_____

_____

_____

_____

_____

_____

Memorable ideas or quotes: _____

_____

_____

_____

_____

_____

_____

_____

_____

_____

_____

_____

_____

RATE THIS BOOK:

Ease of reading: A B C D F

Memorable characters: A B C D F

Originality: A B C D F

Quality of writing: A B C D F

Read other books by this author?   Y or N

Would you read it again?   Y or N

MY BOOK LOG

Date: _____   Overall Grade: **A   B   C   D   F**

Title: _____

Author: _____

My thoughts about this book: _____

_____

_____

_____

_____

_____

_____

_____

Memorable ideas or quotes: _____

_____

_____

_____

_____

_____

_____

_____

_____

_____

_____

_____

_____

RATE THIS BOOK:

Ease of reading: A   B   C   D   F

Memorable characters: A   B   C   D   F

Originality: A   B   C   D   F

Quality of writing: A   B   C   D   F

Read other books by this author?   Y or N

Would you read it again?   Y or N

MY BOOK LOG

Date: _____ Overall Grade: **A   B   C   D   F**

Title: _____

Author: _____

My thoughts about this book: _____

_____

_____

_____

_____

_____

_____

_____

Memorable ideas or quotes: _____

_____

_____

_____

_____

_____

_____

_____

_____

_____

_____

_____

RATE THIS BOOK:

Ease of reading: A   B   C   D   F

Memorable characters: A   B   C   D   F

Originality: A   B   C   D   F

Quality of writing: A   B   C   D   F

Read other books by this author?   Y or N

Would you read it again?   Y or N

MY BOOK LOG

Date: _____ Overall Grade: **A   B   C   D   F**

Title: _____

Author: _____

My thoughts about this book: _____

_____

_____

_____

_____

_____

_____

_____

_____

Memorable ideas or quotes: _____

_____

_____

_____

_____

_____

_____

_____

_____

_____

_____

_____

_____

RATE THIS BOOK:

Ease of reading: A   B   C   D   F

Memorable characters: A   B   C   D   F

Originality: A   B   C   D   F

Quality of writing: A   B   C   D   F

Read other books by this author?   Y or N

Would you read it again?   Y or N

MY BOOK LOG

Date: _____ Overall Grade: **A**   **B**   **C**   **D**   **F**

Title: _____

Author: _____

My thoughts about this book: _____

_____

_____

_____

_____

_____

_____

_____

_____

Memorable ideas or quotes: _____

_____

_____

_____

_____

_____

_____

_____

_____

_____

_____

_____

_____

RATE THIS BOOK:

Ease of reading: A   B   C   D   F

Memorable characters: A   B   C   D   F

Originality: A   B   C   D   F

Quality of writing: A   B   C   D   F

Read other books by this author?   Y or N

Would you read it again?   Y or N

MY BOOK LOG

Date: _____   Overall Grade: **A**   **B**   **C**   **D**   **F**

Title: _____

Author: _____

My thoughts about this book: _____

_____

_____

_____

_____

_____

_____

_____

_____

Memorable ideas or quotes: _____

_____

_____

_____

_____

_____

_____

_____

_____

_____

_____

_____

_____

RATE THIS BOOK:

Ease of reading:	A B C D F
Memorable characters:	A B C D F
Originality:	A B C D F
Quality of writing:	A B C D F

Read other books by this author?   Y or N

Would you read it again?   Y or N

MY BOOK LOG

Date: _____ Overall Grade: **A   B   C   D   F**

Title: _____

Author: _____

My thoughts about this book: _____

_____

_____

_____

_____

_____

_____

_____

_____

Memorable ideas or quotes: _____

_____

_____

_____

_____

RATE THIS BOOK:

Ease of reading: A   B   C   D   F

Memorable characters: A   B   C   D   F

Originality: A   B   C   D   F

Quality of writing: A   B   C   D   F

Read other books by this author?   Y or N

Would you read it again?   Y or N

Date: _____ Overall Grade: **A   B   C   D   F**

Title: _____

Author: _____

My thoughts about this book: _____

_____

_____

_____

_____

_____

_____

_____

_____

Memorable ideas or quotes: _____

_____

_____

_____

_____

RATE THIS BOOK:

Ease of reading: A   B   C   D   F

Memorable characters: A   B   C   D   F

Originality: A   B   C   D   F

Quality of writing: A   B   C   D   F

Read other books by this author?   Y or N

Would you read it again?   Y or N

MY BOOK LOG

Date: _____   Overall Grade: **A   B   C   D   F**

Title: _____

Author: _____

My thoughts about this book: _____

_____

_____

_____

_____

_____

_____

_____

_____

Memorable ideas or quotes: _____

_____

_____

_____

_____

RATE THIS BOOK:

Ease of reading: A B C D F

Memorable characters: A B C D F

Originality: A B C D F

Quality of writing: A B C D F

Read other books by this author? Y or N

Would you read it again? Y or N

MY BOOK LOG

Date: _____ Overall Grade: **A B C D F**

Title: _____

Author: _____

My thoughts about this book: _____

_____

_____

_____

_____

_____

_____

_____

Memorable ideas or quotes: _____

_____

_____

_____

_____

RATE THIS BOOK:

Ease of reading: **A B C D F**

Memorable characters: **A B C D F**

Originality: **A B C D F**

Quality of writing: **A B C D F**

Read other books by this author? **Y** or **N**

Would you read it again? **Y** or **N**

"MAN READING SHOULD BE
MAN INTENSELY ALIVE.
THE BOOK
SHOULD *be a* BALL *of*
LIGHT IN ONE'S HAND."

 — *Ezra Pound*

MEMORABLE QUOTES

**THREE FUNNY WISE MEN ON BOOKS,
BOOKSTORES, AND READING**

Whether we think of them as verbal potted plants or short sentences drawn from long experience, quotations resonate in all of us. Gradually, these memorable snippets become our histories, reminding us that Ralph Waldo Emerson once said that we are all quotations from all our ancestors. Thus, when we jot down a sentence or two or three from a book, we are transplanting it into own experience.

"I find television very educating. Every time somebody turns on the set, I go into the other room and read a book." —Groucho Marx

"Outside of a dog, a book is man's best friend. Inside of a dog it's too dark to read." —Groucho Marx

"From the moment I picked your book up until I laid it down, I convulsed with laughter. Someday I intend reading it." —Groucho Marx

"I took a speed-reading course and read War and Peace in twenty minutes. It involves Russia." —Woody Allen

"I went to a bookstore and asked the saleswoman, 'Where's the self-help section?' She said if she told me, it would defeat the purpose." —George Carlin

"Don't just teach your children to read. Teach them to question what they read. Teach them to question everything." —George Carlin

"

"

Author:

Title:

"

"

Author:

Title:

"

_____

_____

_____

_____

_____

_____

_____

_____

_____

_____

_____

_____

_____

_____

"

Author: _____

Title: _____

"

_____

_____

_____

_____

_____
                                                    "
_____

Author: _____

Title: _____

"
_____

_____

_____

_____

_____
                                                    "
_____

Author: _____

Title: _____

"

_____

_____

_____

_____

_____

_____

_____

_____

_____

_____

_____

_____

"

_____

Author: _____

Title: _____

"SHOW ME A FAMILY OF READERS, AND I WILL SHOW YOU *the* PEOPLE WHO MOVE THE WORLD."

—*Napoleon Bonaparte*

MY FAVORITE BOOKS & AUTHORS

According to a recent compilation, the world's five most popular fiction authors are, in order, William Shakespeare, Agatha Christie, Barbara Cartland, Danielle Steel, and Harold Robbins. In our informal research, however, we quickly discovered that whether you are talking about authors or individual books, popular does not equal favorite. In fact, it didn't take us long to encounter a daunting list of favorite writers and an even more staggering roster of their best books. From Ansel Adams to Émile Zola, these primetime authors just kept coming. As for titles, votes were registered for works by everyone from Herodotus to Gillian Flynn.

Even eccentric books attract enthusiasts. Take, for example, Laurence Sterne's *The Life and Opinions of Tristram Shandy, Gentleman*. Dismissed by some as a digressive, bawdy mess, this lengthy eighteenth-century novel has been embraced by writers and philosophers, including James Joyce, Karl Marx, Salman Rushdie, Carlos Fuentes, and Don DeLillo.

There's no accounting for taste; that's what makes it so interesting. Your choices of favorite authors and books will likely surprise others, and they might even surprise you.

MY FAVORITE BOOKS & AUTHORS

In the section below, jot down your best-regarded or even your most whimsical choices for writers and works.

Title:_____

Author: _____

Why I love this book: _____

_____

_____

Title:_____

Author: _____

Why I love this book: _____

_____

_____

Title: _____

Author: _____

Why I love this book: _____

_____

_____

Title: _____

Author: _____

Why I love this book: _____

_____

_____

Title: _____

Author: _____

Why I love this book: _____

_____

_____

MY FAVORITE BOOKS & AUTHORS

In the section below, jot down your best-regarded or even your most whimsical choices for writers and works.

Title: _____

Author: _____

Why I love this book: _____

_____

_____

Title: _____

Author: _____

Why I love this book: _____

_____

_____

Title: _____

Author: _____

Why I love this book: _____

_____

_____

Title: _____

Author: _____

Why I love this book: _____

_____

_____

Title: _____

Author: _____

Why I love this book: _____

_____

_____

In the section below, jot down your best-regarded or even your most whimsical choices for writers and works.

Title: _____

Author: _____

Why I love this book: _____

_____

_____

Title: _____

Author: _____

Why I love this book: _____

_____

_____

Title: _____

Author: _____

Why I love this book: _____

_____

_____

Title: _____

Author: _____

Why I love this book: _____

_____

_____

Title: _____

Author: _____

Why I love this book: _____

_____

_____

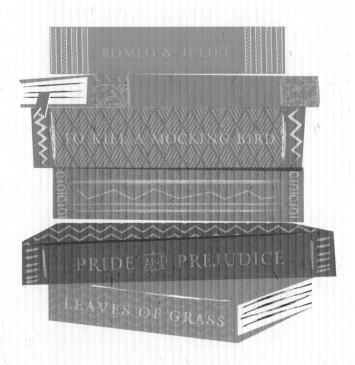

BOOKS THAT CHANGED MY LIFE

Ask a dozen people what books changed their lives (we did), and you will likely receive at least that many different answers. For some people, it could be a children's book or a high school chemistry text; for others, a diet guide that worked, a translation of Dante's *Divine Comedy*, or Mitch Albom's *Tuesdays with Morrie*. One person credited *The Rough Guide to Morocco* with helping him overcome his fear of travel, even as another insisted quite seriously that Dr. Seuss' *Oh, The Places You'll Go!* prepared her for her future—"even if it was then just in grade school."

One inveterate reader told us that he became a writer partly because of, all things, James Boswell's *Life of Samuel Johnson*. Robert Pirsig's philosophical novel *Zen and the Art of Motorcycle Maintenance* and Jack Kerouac's classic *On the Road* are documented to have convinced more than a few college students to refocus their lives.

Authors sometimes find their own life-changing reading in unexpected sources. Mary Higgins Clark is a perennial bestselling mystery writer, but she told an interviewer that it was a reading of Pearl Buck's *The Good Earth*, when she was nine, that convinced her to be a writer. For Alice McDermott, the inspiration came from the maudlin manuscripts that she had to read while working as an editor for a vanity publisher.

What books (note the plural) have set you on a refreshing life path or gifted you with a newfound tranquility?

In the space below, jot down your own selections for life-changing reading.

Title: _____

Author: _____

Why this book is important to me and how it changed me:

_____

_____

_____

_____

Title: _____

Author: _____

Why this book is important to me and how it changed me:

_____

_____

_____

_____

Title: _____

Author: _____

Why this book is important to me and how it changed me:

_____

_____

_____

_____

Title: _____

Author: _____

Why this book is important to me and how it changed me:

_____

_____

_____

_____

Title:_____

Author: _____

Why this book is important to me and how it changed me:

_____

_____

_____

_____

Title:_____

Author: _____

Why this book is important to me and how it changed me:

_____

_____

_____

_____

Title: _____

Author: _____

Why this book is important to me and how it changed me:

_____

_____

_____

_____

Title: _____

Author: _____

Why this book is important to me and how it changed me:

_____

_____

_____

_____

"THE READING OF ALL GOOD BOOKS *is like a* CONVERSATION *with the most* EMINENT PEOPLE *of* PAST CENTURIES...**"**

—*René Descartes*

LITERARY PILGRIMAGES

Visiting the former home of a beloved author can give even the most ardent devotee a deeper sense of who the writer was and how he or she lived. In compiling this gathering of literary landmarks, we metaphorically walked the extra mile to seek destinations that offered more than just a plaque or an apology that the original building had been replaced by a rug store or pie shop. Each of our selections offers not only the immediate context of place, but also an enhanced sense of the author who lived there.

One additional tip: Each of these landmarks is multifaceted. Most of them have guided tours, many feature additional events, several have gift stores, and all of them have informative websites with directions.

~~~~~~~~~~~~~~~~~~~~~~

JACK LONDON STATE HISTORIC PARK, 2400 London Ranch Road, Glen Ellen, California 95442. (707) 938-5216

NATIONAL STEINBECK CENTER, 1 Main Street, Salinas, California 93901. (831) 775-4721

THE ERNEST HEMINGWAY HOME & MUSEUM, 907 Whitehead Street, Key West, Florida 33040. (305) 294-1136.

MARGARET MITCHELL HOUSE, 990 Peachtree Street NE, Atlanta, Georgia 30309. (404) 249-7015

ERNEST HEMINGWAY BIRTHPLACE AND MUSEUM, 200 North Oak Park Avenue, Oak Park, Illinois 60303. (708) 445-3071 and (708) 524-5383

THE KURT VONNEGUT MEMORIAL LIBRARY, The Emelie Building, 340 North Senate Avenue, Indianapolis, Indiana 46204. (317) 652-1954

THE EMILY DICKINSON MUSEUM, 280 Main Street, Amherst, Massachusetts 01002. (413) 542-8161

THE WAYSIDE, HOME OF THE HAWTHORNES AND THE ALCOTTS, Minuteman National Historical Park, 455 Lexington Road, Concord, Massachusetts 01742. (978) 318-7825

THE MOUNT, EDITH WHARTON'S HOME, 2 Plunkett Street, Lenox, Massachusetts 02140. (413) 551-5111

HERMAN MELVILLE'S ARROWHEAD, 780 Holmes Road, Pittsfield, Massachusetts 01201. (413) 442-1793

THE MARK TWAIN BOYHOOD HOME & MUSEUM, North Main Street, Hannibal, Missouri 63401. (573) 221-9010

THE LAURA INGALLS WILDER HISTORIC HOME & MUSEUM, 3068 Highway A, Mansfield, Missouri. (877) 924-7126

WILLA CATHER BIRTHPLACE, 413 North Webster, Red Cloud, Nebraska 68970. (866) 731-7304

THE WALT WHITMAN BIRTHPLACE HISTORIC SITE,
246 Old Whitman Road, Huntington Station, New York 11476.
(631) 427-5240

CHARLES DICKENS HOME AND MUSEUM, 48 Doughty Street,
London WC1N 2LX, United Kingdom. +44 20 7405 2127

THE SHERLOCK HOLMES MUSEUM, 221b Baker Street,
London NW1 6XE, United Kingdom. +44 207 224 3688

THE SHAKESPEARE BIRTHPLACE TRUST,
The Shakespeare Centre, Henley Street,
Stratford Upon Avon, Warwickshire CV37 6QW. +44 1789 20401

A SELECTION OF BOOKSTORES WORTH VISITING

"I have gone to them [bookshops] for years,
always finding the one book I wanted—
and then three more I hadn't known I wanted."
  —MARY ANN SHAFFER

"A book worth reading is worth buying."
  —JOHN RUSKIN

"Where is human nature so weak as in a bookstore?"
  —HENRY WARD BEECHER

An anonymous sage once said that it's not surprising that many romantic relationships begin in bookstores because so many other meaningful connections are formed there. Many of us can still remember the shop where we first picked up a copy of *The Joy of Cooking* or thumbed through our first novel by David Baldacci, J. K. Rowling, or Sue Grafton. Those first bookstore encounters were the beginnings of long, important relationships that have outlasted many marriages.

This gathering of notable bookstores is eclectic, personal, sometimes whimsical, and definitely not final or exclusionary. For each state and the District of Columbia, two bookstores were selected, to which a smattering of overseas bookshops were added. The bookstores were chosen because their selection and local staff help generate interest among area booklovers. These independents and chain stores share a sense of purpose in bolstering a community of readers. Mercifully, they are not alone: this list could be doubled and redoubled and redoubled again. Bookstores nurture us in ways that nothing else does.

JIM REED BOOKS. 2021 3rd Avenue N.,
Birmingham, Alabama 35203. (205) 326-4460

BIENVILLE BOOKS, 109 Dauphin Street,
Mobile, Alabama 36602. (251) 438.2904

TITLE WAVE BOOKS, 1360 W. Northern Lights Boulevard,
Anchorage, Alaska 99503. (904) 278-9283

FAIRBANKS BARNES & NOBLE, 421 Mehar Avenue,
Fairbanks, Alaska 99701. (907) 452-6400

METRO BARNES & NOBLE, Metro Center,
10235 North Metro Parkway East,
Phoenix, Arizona 85051. (602) 678-0088

CHANGING HANDS BOOKSTORE,
6428 South McClintock Drive, Tempe, Arizona 85283.
(480) 730-0205

DICKSON STREET BOOKSHOP, 325 West Dickson Street,
Fayetteville, Arkansas 72701. (479) 442-8182

WORDSWORTH BOOKS & CO., 5920 R Street,
Little Rock, Arkansas 72207. (501) 663-9198

THE GROVE AT FARMERS MARKET BARNES & NOBLE,
189 The Grove Drive, Suite K30,
Los Angeles, California 90036. (323) 525-0270

VROMAN'S BOOKSTORE, 695 E. Colorado Blvd.,
Pasadena, California 91101. (626) 449-5320

BOULDER BOOK STORE, 1107 Pearl Street,
Boulder, Colorado 80302. (303) 447-2074

THE BOOKIES, 4315 East Mississippi Avenue,
Denver, Colorado 80246. (303) 759-1117

ATTICUS, 1082 Chapel Street,
New Haven, Connecticut 06510. (203) 776-4040

THE BOOK BARN, 41 West Main Street,
Niantic, Connecticut 06357. (860) 739-5715

CAPTAIN BLUE HEN COMICS & ENTERTAINMENT, 80 East Main
Street, Suite 101, Newark, Delaware 19711. (302) 737-3434

CHRISTIANA MALL BARNES & NOBLE, 340 Christiana Mall,
Newark, Delaware 19702. (302) 369-7050

THE BOOKSTORE IN THE GROVE, 3390 Mary Street,
Coconut Grove, Florida 33133. (305) 443-2855

COLONIAL DRIVE BARNES & NOBLE, 2418 East Colonial Drive,
Orlando, Florida 32803. (407) 894-6024

BOUND TO READ BOOKS, 481 Flat Shoals Avenue,
Atlanta, Georgia 30316. (404) 522-0877

EAGLE EYE BOOK SHOP, 2076 North Decatur Road,
Decatur, Georgia 30033. (404) 486-0307

JELLY'S, 98-023 Hekaha Street, Aiea, Hawaii. (808) 484-4413

ALA MOANA BARNES & NOBLE, 1450 Ala Moana Boulevard,
Honolulu, Hawaii 96814. (808) 949-7307

BOISE BARNES & NOBLE, 1301 North Milwaukee Street,
Boise, Idaho 83704. (208) 375-4454

CHAPTER ONE BOOKSTORE, 340 East Second Street,
Ketchum, Idaho 83340. (208) 726-5425

MYOPIC BOOKS, 1564 North Milwaukee Avenue,
Chicago, Illinois 60622. (773) 862-4882

UNABRIDGED BOOKS, 3251 North Broadway,
Chicago, Illinois 60657. (773) 883-9119

HALF PRICE BOOKSTORE, 4709 East 82nd Street,
Indianapolis, Indiana 46250. (317) 577-0410

INDIE READS BOOKS, 911 Massachusetts Avenue,
Indianapolis, Indiana 46202. (317) 384-1496

HALF PRICE BOOKS, 1400 Twixt Town Road NE,
Cedar Rapids, Iowa 52302. (319) 377-4982

PRAIRIE LIGHTS BOOKSTORE, 15 South Dubuque Street,
Iowa City, Iowa 52240. (319) 337-2681

RAINY DAY BOOKS, 2706 West 53rd Street,
Fairway, Kansas 66205. (913) 384-3126

WATERMARK BOOKS & CAFÉ, 4701 East Douglas,
Wichita, Kansas 67218. (316) 682-1181

JOSEPH-BETH BOOKSELLERS, 61 Lexington Green Center, Suite B1,
Lexington, Kentucky 40503. (859) 273-2911

CARMICHAEL'S BOOKSTORE, 1295 Bardstown Road,
Louisville, Kentucky 40204. (502) 456-6950

FAULKNER HOUSE BOOKS, 624 Pirates Alley,
New Orleans, Louisiana 70116. (504) 524-2940

SHREVEPORT BARNES & NOBLE, Bayou Walk, 6646 Youree Drive,
Shreveport, Louisiana 71105. (318) 798-6066

MARKETPLACE DRIVE BARNES & NOBLE, 9 Marketplace Drive,
Augusta, Maine 04330. (207) 621-0038

GULF OF MAINE BOOKS, 34 Maine Street,
Brunswick, Maine 04011. (207) 729-5083

THE IVY, 6080 Falls Road,
Baltimore, Maryland 21209. (410) 377-2966

KELMSCOTT BOOKSHOP, 34 W. 25th Street,
Baltimore, Maryland 21218. (410) 235-6810

THE COOP, 1400 Massachusetts Avenue,
Cambridge, Massachusetts 02139. (617) 499-2000

BAKER BOOKS, 2 McCabe Street,
Dartmouth, Massachusetts 02747. (508) 997-6700

ANN ARBOR BARNES & NOBLE, Huron Village, 3235 Washtenaw
Avenue, Ann Arbor, Michigan 48104. (734) 973-0846

JOHN K. KING USED & RARE BOOKS, 901 West Lafayette
Boulevard, Detroit, Michigan 48226. (313) 961-0622.

ONCE UPON A CRIME, 604 West Street,
Minneapolis, Minnesota 55405. (612) 870-3785

ROSEVILLE II BARNES & NOBLE, HarMar Mall, 2100 North Snelling
Avenue, Roseville, Minnesota 55113. (651) 639-9256

SQUARE BOOKS, 160 Courthouse Square,
Oxford, Mississippi 38655. (662) 236-2262

LORELEI BOOKS, 1103 Washington Street,
Vicksburg, Mississippi 39183. (601) 634-8624

KANSAS CITY BARNES & NOBLE, 400 West 47th Street,
Kansas City, Missouri 64112. (816) 753-1313

SUBTERRANEAN BOOKS, 6275 Delmar Boulevard,
St. Louis, Missouri 63130. (314) 862-6100

COUNTRY BOOKSHELF, 28 West Main,
Bozeman, Montana 59715. (406) 587-0166

BOOKSTORE AT THE UNIVERSITY OF MONTANA,
Mountain Campus, University Center, 5 Campus Drive,
Missoula, Montana 59801. (406) 243-1234

HAYMARKET CREAMERY BUILDING, 701 P Street, Suite 102,
Lincoln, Nebraska. (402) 477-7770

JACKSON STREET BOOKSELLERS, 1119 Jackson Street,
Omaha, Nebraska. (402) 341-2664

NORTHWEST BARNES & NOBLE, Rainbow Promenade, 2191 North
Rainbow Boulevard, Las Vegas, Nevada 89108. (702) 631-1775

SUNDANCE BOOKS AND MUSIC, 121 California Avenue,
Reno, Nevada 89509. (775) 786-1188

GIBSON'S BOOKSTORE, 45 South Maine Street,
Concord, New Hampshire 03301. (603) 224-0562

THE TOADSTOOL BOOKSHOP, 12 Depot Square,
Peterborough, New Hampshire 03458. (603) 924-3543

PARAMUS BARNES & NOBLE, 765 Route 17 South,
Paramus, New Jersey 07652. (201) 445-4589

THE TOWN BOOKSTORE, 270 East Broad Street,
Westfield, New Jersey 07090. (908) 233-3535

BOOKWORKS, 4022 Rio Grande Blvd NW,
Albuquerque, New Mexico 87107. (505) 344-8139

PAGE 1 BOOKSTORE, 5850 Eubank Blvd NE, Unit #B41,
Albuquerque, New Mexico 87111. (505) 294-2026

THE STRAND BOOKSTORE, 828 Broadway,
New York, New York 10003. (212) 473-1452

UNION SQUARE BARNES & NOBLE, 33 East 17th Street,
New York, New York 10003. (212) 253-0810

MALAPROPS BOOKSTORE & CAFÉ, 55 Haywood Street,
Asheville, North Carolina 28801. (828) 254-6734

MORRISON PLACE BARNES & NOBLE, 4020 Sharon Road,
Charlotte, North Carolina 28211. (704) 364-0626

FARGO BARNES & NOBLE, 1201 42 Street SW,
Fargo, North Dakota 58103. (701) 281-1002

MAIN STREET BOOKS, 106 Main Street South,
Minot, North Dakota 58701. (701) 839-4050

FIRESIDE BOOK SHOP, 29 North Franklin Street,
Chagrin Falls, Ohio 44022. (440) 247-4050

THE BOOK LOFT OF GERMAN VILLAGE, 631 South Third Street,
Columbus, Ohio 43206. (614) 464-1774

FULL CIRCLE BOOKSTORE, 50 Penn Place, 1900 NW Expressway,
Oklahoma City, Oklahoma 73118. (405) 842-2900

MAY AVENUE BARNES & NOBLE, 6100 North May Avenue,
Oklahoma City, Oklahoma 73112. (405) 843-9300

EUGENE BARNES & NOBLE, 163 Valley River Drive,
Eugene, Oregon 97401. (541) 687-0356

POWELL'S CITY OF BOOKS, 1005 West Burnside Street,
Portland, Oregon 97209. (503) 228-4651

RITTENHOUSE SQUARE BARNES & NOBLE, 1805 Walnut Street,
Philadelphia, Pennsylvania 19103. (215) 665-0716

THE SPIRAL BOOKCASE, 112 Cotton Street,
Philadelphia, Pennsylvania 19127. (215) 482-0704

THE STUDIO AT BARRINGTON BOOKS, 184 Country Road, Barrington, Rhode Island 02806. (401) 245-7925

CELLAR STORIES BOOK STORE, 11 Mathewson Street, Providence, Rhode Island 02903. (401) 521-2665

BEAUFORT BOOKSTORE, 2127 Boundary Street, Beaufort, South Carolina 29902. (843) 525-1066

HUB CITY BOOKSTORE, 186 West Main Street, Spartanburg, South Carolina 29306. (864) 577-9349

BLACK HILLS BOOKS AND TREASURES, 112 South Chicago Street, Hot Springs, South Dakota 57747. (605) 745-5545

ZANDBROZ VARIETY, 209 South Phillips Avenue, Sioux City, South Dakota 57104. (605) 331-5137

BOOK STOP PLUS, 2810 Bartlett Road, Suite 8, Memphis, Tennessee 38134. (901) 382-222

GERMANTOWN PARKWAY BARNES & NOBLE, 2774 North Germantown Parkway, Memphis, Tennessee 38133. (901) 386-2468

LINCOLN PARK BARNES & NOBLE, 7700 West Northwest Highway, Suite 300, Dallas, Texas 75225. (214) 739-1124

BRAZOS BOOKSTORE, 2421 Bissonnet Street, Houston, Texas 77005. (713) 523-0701

GATEWAY BARNES & NOBLE, 6 North Rio Grande Street, Salt Lake City, Utah 84101. (801) 456-0100

WELLER BOOK WORKS, 607 Trolley Square, Salt Lake City, Utah 84102. (801) 328-2586

NORTHSHIRE BOOKSTORE, 4869 Main Street, Manchester Center, Vermont 05255. (602) 362-2200

BOXCAR & CABOOSE, 394 Railroad Street, Suite 2,
St. Johnsbury, Vermont 05819. (802) 748-3551

MCKAY USED BOOKS, 8345 Sudley Road,
Manassas, Virginia 20109. (703) 361-9042

PRINCE BOOKS, 109 East Main Street,
Norfolk, Virginia 23510. (757) 622-9223

ELLIOTT BAY BOOKSTORE, 1521 Tenth Avenue,
Seattle, Washington 98122. (206) 624-6600

MAGUS USED BOOKS, 408 NE 42nd Street,
Seattle, Washington 98105. (206) 633-1800

CAPITOL HILL BOOKS, 657 C Street SE,
Washington, D.C. 20003. (202) 544-1621

DOWNTOWN D.C. BARNES & NOBLE, 555 12th Street NW,
Washington, D.C. 20004. (202) 347-0176

MAINLINE BOOKSTORE, 301 Davis Avenue,
Elkins, West Virginia 26241. (304) 636-6770

WORDS & MUSIC BOOKSHOP, 4 Hyde Park Drive,
Wheeling, West Virginia 26003. (304) 232-6539

GREENFIELD PLACE, 5032 South 74th Street,
Greenfield, Wisconsin 53220. (414) 281-0000

A ROOM OF ONE'S OWN, 315 West Gorham Street,
Madison, Wisconsin 53703. (608) 257-7888

VALLEY BOOKSTORE, 125 North Cache Drive,
Jackson, Wyoming 83001. (307) 733-4533

MAD DOG AND THE PILGRIM BOOKSELLERS, 4176 Highway 789,
Sweetwater Station, Wyoming 82520. (307) 544-2203

...And half a dozen other world-class English-language bookstores in other parts of the world:

GOULD'S BOOK ARCADE, 32 King Street, Newtown, 2042, New South Wales, Australia. +61 2 9519-8947

MUNRO'S BOOKS, 108 Government Street, Victoria, British Columbia, Canada V8W 1Y2. (250) 382-2464

SHAKESPEARE AND COMPANY, 37 rue de la Bûcherie, 75005 Paris, France. +33 (0) 1-43-25-40-93

CHARLIE BYRNE'S BOOKSHOP, The Cornstore, Middle Street, Galway, Ireland. +353 (0) 91561766

DAUNT BOOKS MARYLEBONE, 83 Marylebone High Street, London W1U 4QW, United Kingdom. +44 20 7224 2295

FOYLE'S AT CHARING CROSS, 113–119 Charing Cross Road, London WC2H 0EB, United Kingdom. +44 20 7437 5660

...And, for good measure, an entire town of bookstores: Hay-on-Wye in Wales.

"DO NOT READ,
as CHILDREN DO, *to*
AMUSE YOURSELF,
or like the AMBITIOUS,
FOR THE PURPOSE
of INSTRUCTION.
NO, READ IN
ORDER *to* LIVE."

— *Gustave Flaubert*

VERY CLICKABLE BOOK WEBSITES

For the digitally inclined, here's a baker's dozen of delectable book sites:

Abebooks. www.abebooks.com

Alibris. www.alibris.com

Amazon. www.amazon.com

Barnes & Noble. www.barnesandnoble.com

Betterworldbooks. www.betterworldbooks.com

Bookfinder. www.bookfinder.com

Bookriot. www.bookriot.com

GoodReads. www.goodreads.com

Library Thing. www.librarything.com

Shelfari. www.shelfari.com

The Millions. www.themillions.com

The Staff Recommends. www.thestaffrecommends.com

Tomfolio. www.tomfolio.com

In addition to this batch, all of the bookstores and literary pilgrimages listed in previous sections maintain websites worthy of your attention.

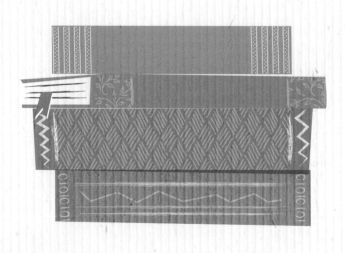

AWARD-WINNING BOOKS AND AUTHORS

Book that are considered to be the best don't spoil or lose their luster. Early works by Alice Walker or Anne Tyler, or even Jane Austen and Virginia Woolf, somehow retain their magic decades, or even centuries, later. Thus, lists of noteworthy or award-winning books from the past aren't just empty cavalcades of brittle history, but bountiful fields waiting to be harvested.

In that spirit, gathered here are several of the most significant award groupings. Because of limited space, only selections from 1980 to the present are listed for the following:

- **The Modern Library 100 best twentieth-century novels and nonfiction**
- **The National Book Award for fiction and nonfiction**
- **The Pulitzer Prize for fiction and nonfiction**
- **The Man Booker Prize**
- **The Nobel Prize in Literature**
- **The New York Public Library's most borrowed books**
- **Oprah's Book Club**
- **Oprah's Book Club 2.0**

THE MODERN LIBRARY'S 100 BEST NOVELS

1. *Ulysses* by James Joyce
2. *The Great Gatsby* by F. Scott Fitzgerald
3. *A Portrait of the Artist as a Young Man* by James Joyce
4. *Lolita* by Vladimir Nabokov
5. *Brave New World* by Aldous Huxley
6. *The Sound and the Fury* by William Faulkner
7. *Catch-22* by Joseph Heller
8. *Darkness at Noon* by Arthur Koestler
9. *Sons and Lovers* by D. H. Lawrence
10. *The Grapes of Wrath by John Steinbeck*
11. *Under the Volcano* by Malcolm Lowry
12. *The Way of All Flesh* by Samuel Butler
13. *1984* by George Orwell
14. *I, Claudius* by Robert Graves
15. *To the Lighthouse* by Virginia Woolf
16. *An American Tragedy* by Theodore Dreiser
17. *The Heart Is a Lonely Hunter* by Carson McCullers
18. *Slaughterhouse-Five* by Kurt Vonnegut
19. *Invisible Man* by Ralph Ellison
20. *Native Son* by Richard Wright
21. *Henderson the Rain King* by Saul Bellow
22. *Appointment in Samarra* by John O'Hara
23. *U.S.A.* (trilogy) by John Dos Passos
24. *Winesburg, Ohio* by Sherwood Anderson
25. *A Passage to India* by E. M. Forster
26. *The Wings of the Dove* by Henry James
27. *The Ambassadors* by Henry James
28. *Tender Is the Night* by F. Scott Fitzgerald
29. *The Studs Lonigan Trilogy* by James T. Farrell
30. *The Good Soldier* by Ford Madox Ford
31. *Animal Farm* by George Orwell
32. *The Golden Bowl* by Henry James

33. *Sister Carrie* by Theodore Dreiser

34. *A Handful of Dust* by Evelyn Waugh

35. *As I Lay Dying* by William Faulkner

36. *All the King's Men* by Robert Penn Warren

37. *The Bridge of San Luis Rey* by Thornton Wilder

38. *Howard's End* by E. M. Forster

39. *Go Tell It on the Mountain* by James Baldwin

40. *The Heart of the Matter* by Graham Greene

41. *Lord of the Flies* by William Golding

42. *Deliverance* by James Dickey

43. *A Dance to the Music of Time* (series) by Anthony Powell

44. *Point Counter Point* by Aldous Huxley

45. *The Sun Also Rises* by Ernest Hemingway

46. *The Secret Agent* by Joseph Conrad

47. *Nostromo* by Joseph Conrad

48. *The Rainbow* by D. H. Lawrence

49. *Women in Love* by D. H. Lawrence

50. *Tropic of Cancer* by Henry Miller

51. *The Naked and the Dead* by Norman Mailer

52. *Portnoy's Complaint* by Philip Roth

53. *Pale Fire* by Vladimir Nabokov

54. *Light in August* by William Faulkner

55. *On the Road* by Jack Kerouac

56. *The Maltese Falcon* by Dashiell Hammett

57. *Parade's End* by Ford Madox Ford

58. *The Age of Innocence* by Edith Wharton

59. *Zuleika Dobson* by Max Beerbohm

60. *The Moviegoer* by Walker Percy

61. *Death Comes for the Archbishop* by Willa Cather

62. *From Here to Eternity* by James Jones

63. *The Wapshot Chronicles* by John Cheever

64. *The Catcher in the Rye* by J. D. Salinger

65. *A Clockwork Orange* by Anthony Burgess

66. *Of Human Bondage* by W. Somerset Maugham

67. *Heart of Darkness* by Joseph Conrad

68. *Main Street* by Sinclair Lewis

69. *The House of Mirth* by Edith Wharton

70. *The Alexandria Quartet* by Lawrence Durell

71. *A High Wind in Jamaica* by Richard Hughes

72. *A House For Mr. Biswas* by V. S. Naipaul

73. *The Day of the Locust* by Nathanael West

74. *A Farewell to Arms* by Ernest Hemingway

75. *Scoop* by Evelyn Waugh

76. *The Prime of Miss Jean Brodie* by Muriel Spark

77. *Finnegans Wake* by James Joyce

78. *Kim* by Rudyard Kipling

79. *A Room with a View* by E. M. Forster

80. *Brideshead Revisited* by Evelyn Waugh

81. *The Adventures of Augie March* by Saul Bellow

82. *Angle of Repose* by Wallace Stegner

83. *A Bend in the River* by V. S. Naipaul

84. *The Death of the Heart* by Elizabeth Bowen

85. *Lord Jim* by Joseph Conrad

86. *Ragtime* by E. L. Doctorow

87. *The Old Wives' Tale* by Arnold Bennett

88. *The Call of the Wild* by Jack London

89. *Loving* by Henry Green

90. *Midnight's Children* by Salman Rushdie

91. *Tobacco Road* by Erskine Caldwell

92. *Ironweed* by William Kennedy

93. *The Magus* by John Fowles

94. *Wide Sargasso Sea* by Jean Rhys

95. *Under the Net* by Iris Murdoch

96. *Sophie's Choice* by William Styron

97. *The Sheltering Sky* by Paul Bowles

98. *The Postman Always Rings Twice* by James M. Cain

99. *The Ginger Man* by J. P. Donleavy

100. *The Magnificent Ambersons* by Booth Tarkington

THE MODERN LIBRARY'S 100 BEST NONFICTION

1. *The Education of Henry Adams* by Henry Adams
2. *The Varieties of Religious Experience* by William James
3. *Up from Slavery* by Booker T. Washington
4. *A Room of One's Own* by Virginia Woolf
5. *Silent Spring* by Rachel Carson
6. *Selected Essays, 1917–1932* by T. S. Eliot
7. *The Double Helix* by James D. Watson
8. *Speak, Memory* by Vladimir Nabokov
9. *The American Language* by H. L. Mencken
10. *The General Theory of Employment, Interest, and Money* by John Maynard Keynes
11. *The Lives of a Cell* by Lewis Thomas
12. *The Frontier in American History* by Frederick Jackson Turner
13. *Black Boy* by Richard Wright
14. *Aspects of the Novel* by E. M. Forster
15. *The Civil War* by Shelby Foote
16. *The Guns of August* by Barbara Tuchman
17. *The Proper Study of Mankind* by Isaiah Berlin
18. *The Nature and Destiny of Man* by Reinhold Niebuhr
19. *Notes of a Native Son* by James Baldwin
20. *The Autobiography of Alice B. Toklas* by Gertrude Stein
21. *The Elements of Style* by William Strunk and E. B. White
22. *An American Dilemma* by Gunnar Myrdal
23. *Principia Mathematica* by Alfred North Whitehead and Bertrand Russell
24. *The Mismeasure of Man* by Stephen Jay Gould
25. *The Mirror and the Lamp* by Meyer Howard Abrams
26. *The Art of the Soluble* by Peter B. Medawar
27. *The Ants* by Bert Hölldobler and Edward O. Wilson
28. *A Theory of Justice* by John Rawls
29. *Art and Illusion* by Ernest H. Gombrich
30. *The Making of the English Working Class* by E. P. Thompson

98. *The Taming of Chance* by Ian Hacking
99. *Operating Instructions* by Anne Lamott
100. *Melbourne* by Lord David Cecil

~~~~~~~~~~~~~~~

THE NATIONAL BOOK AWARD FOR FICTION

1980. *Sophie's Choice* by William Styron
1981. *Plains Song* by Wright Morris
1982. *Rabbit Is Rich* by John Updike
1983. *The Color Purple* by Alice Walker
1984. *Victory Over Japan: A Book of Stories* by Ellen Gilchrist
1985. *White Noise* by Don DeLillo
1986. *World's Fair* by E. L. Doctorow
1987. *Paco's Story* by Larry Heinemann
1988. *Paris Trout* by Pete Dexter
1989. *Spartina* by John Casey
1990. *Middle Passage* by Charles Johnson
1991. *Mating* by Norman Rush
1992. *All the Pretty Horses* by Cormac McCarthy
1993. *The Shipping News* by E. Annie Proulx
1994. *A Frolic of His Own* by William Gaddis
1995. *Sabbath's Theater* by Philip Roth
1996. *Ship Fever and Other Stories* by Andrea Barrett
1997. *Cold Mountain* by Charles Frazier
1998. *Charming Billy* by Alice McDermott
1999. *Waiting* by Ha Jin
2000. *In America* by Susan Sontag
2001. *The Corrections* by Jonathan Franzen
2002. *Three Junes* by Julia Glass
2003. *The Great Fire* by Shirley Hazzard
2004. *The News from Paraguay* by Lily Tuck
2005. *Europe Central* by William T. Vollmann

2006. *The Echo Maker* by Richard Powers
2007. *Tree of Smoke* by Denis Johnson
2008. *Shadow Country* by Peter Matthiessen
2009. *Let the Great World Spin* by Colum McCann
2010. *Lord of Misrule* by Jaimy Gordon
2011. *Salvage the Bones* by Jesmyn Ward
2012. *The Round House* by Louise Erdrich
2013. *The Good Lord Bird* by James McBride

THE NATIONAL BOOK AWARD FOR HISTORY

1980. *The White House Years* by Henry A. Kissinger
1981. *Christianity, Social Tolerance, and Homosexuality*
        by John Boswell
1982. *People of the Sacred Mountain: A History of the Northern
        Cheyenne Chiefs and Warrior Societies, 1830–1879*
        by Father Peter John Powell
1983. *Voices of Protest: Huey Long, Father Coughlin,
        and the Great Depression* by Alan Brinkley

THE NATIONAL BOOK AWARD FOR SCIENCE

1980. *Gödel, Escher, Bach: An Eternal Golden Braid*
        by Douglas Hofstadter
1981. *The Panda's Thumb: More Reflections on Natural History*
        by Stephen Jay Gould
1982. *Lucy: The Beginnings of Humankind*
        by Donald C. Johanson & Maitland A. Edey
1983. *Subtle Is the Lord: The Science and Life of Albert Einstein*
        by Abraham Pais

THE NATIONAL BOOK AWARD FOR NONFICTION

2004. *Arc of Justice: A Saga of Race, Civil Rights, and Murder in the Jazz Age* by Kevin Boyle

2005. *The Year of Magical Thinking* by Joan Didion

2006. *The Worst Hard Time: The Untold Story of Those Who Survived the Great American Dust Bowl* by Timothy Egan

2007. *Legacy of Ashes: The History of the CIA* by Tim Weiner

2008. *The Hemingses of Monticello: An American Family* by Annette Gordon-Reed

2009. *The First Tycoon: The Epic Life of Cornelius Vanderbilt* by T. J. Stiles

2010. *Just Kids* by Patti Smith

2011. *The Swerve: How the World Became Modern* by Stephen Greenblatt

2012. *Behind the Beautiful Forevers: Life, Death, and Hope in a Mumbai Undercity* by Katherine Boo

2013. *The Unwinding: An Inner History of the New America* by George Packer

~~~~~~~~~~~~

THE PULITZER PRIZE FOR FICTION

1980. *The Executioner's Song* by Norman Mailer

1981. *A Confederacy of Dunces* by John Kennedy Toole

1982. *Rabbit Is Rich* by John Updike

1983. *The Color Purple* by Alice Walker

1984. *Ironweed* by William Kennedy

1985. *Foreign Affairs* by Alison Lurie

1986. *Lonesome Dove* by Larry McMurtry

1987. *A Summons to Memphis* by Peter Taylor

1988. *Beloved* by Toni Morrison

1989. *Breathing Lessons* by Anne Tyler

1990. *The Mambo Kings Play Songs of Love* by Oscar Hijuelos

1991. *Rabbit at Rest* by John Updike

1992. *A Thousand Acres* by Jane Smiley

1993. *A Good Scent from a Strange Mountain* by Robert Olen Butler

1994. *The Shipping News* by E. Annie Proulx

1995. *The Stone Diaries* by Carol Shields

1996. *Independence Day* by Richard Ford

1997. *Martin Dressler: The Tale of an American Dreamer*
   by Steven Millhauser

1998. *American Pastoral* by Philip Roth

1999. *The Hours* by Michael Cunningham

2000. *Interpreter of Maladies* by Jhumpa Lahiri

2001. *The Amazing Adventures of Kavalier & Clay*
   by Michael Chabon

2002. *Empire Falls* by Richard Russo

2003. *Middlesex* by Jeffrey Eugenides

2004. *The Known World* by Edward P. Jones

2005. *Gilead* by Marilynne Robinson

2006. *March* by Geraldine Brooks

2007. *The Road* by Cormac McCarthy

2008. *The Brief Wondrous Life of Oscar Wao* by Junot Díaz

2009. *Olive Kitteridge* by Elizabeth Strout

2010. *Tinkers* by Paul Harding

2011. *A Visit From the Goon Squad* by Jennifer Egan

2012. No award given.

2013. *The Orphan Master's Son* by Adam Johnson

2014. *The Goldfinch* by Donna Tartt

~~~~~~~~~~~

THE PULITZER PRIZE FOR GENERAL NONFICTION

1980. *Gödel, Escher, Bach: An Eternal Golden Braid*
   by Douglas Hofstadter

1981. *Fin-de-Siècle Vienna: Politics and Culture* by Carl E. Schorske

1982. *The Soul of a New Machine* by Tracy Kidder

1983. *Is There No Place on Earth for Me?* by Susan Sheehan

1984. *The Social Transformation of American Medicine*
   by Paul Starr

1985. *The Good War: An Oral History of World War Two* by Studs Terkel

1986. (two winners) *Common Ground: A Turbulent Decade in the Lives of Three American Families* by J. Anthony Lukas and *Move Your Shadow: South Africa, Black and White* by Joseph Lelyveld

1987. *Arab and Jew: Wounded Spirits in a Promised Land* by David K. Shipler

1988. *The Making of the Atomic Bomb* by Richard Rhodes

1989. *A Bright Shining Lie: John Paul Vann and America in Vietnam* by Neil Sheehan

1990. *And Their Children After Them* by Dale Maharidge and Michael Williamson

1991. *The Ants* by Bert Hölldobler and Edward O. Wilson

1992. *The Prize: The Epic Quest for Oil, Money, andPower* by Daniel Yergin

1993. *Lincoln at Gettysburg: The Words That Remade America* by Garry Wills

1994. *Lenin's Tomb: The Last Days of the Soviet Empire* by David Remnick

1995. *The Beak of the Finch: A Story of Evolution in Our Time* by Jonathan Weiner

1996. *The Haunted Land: Facing Europe's Ghosts After Communism* by Tina Rosenberg

1997. *Ashes to Ashes: America's Hundred-Year Cigarette War, the Public Health, and the Unabashed Triumph of Philip Morris* by Richard Kluger

1998. *Guns, Germs, and Steel: The Fates of Human Societies* by Jared Diamond

1999. *Annals of the Former World* by John McPhee

2000. *Embracing Defeat: Japan in the Wake of World War II* by John W. Dower

2001. *Hirohito and the Making of Modern Japan* by Herbert P. Bix

2002. *Carry Me Home: Birmingham, Alabama, the Climactic Battle of the Civil Rights Revolution* by Diane McWhorter

~~~~~~~~~~

THE PULITZER PRIZE FOR HISTORY

1984. No award given.

1985. *Prophets of Regulation* by Thomas K. McCraw

1986. *...the Heavens and the Earth: A Political History of the Space Age* by Walter A. McDougall

1987. *Voyagers to the West: A Passage in the Peopling of America on the Eve of the Revolution* by Bernard Bailyn

1988. *The Launching of Modern American Science, 1846-1876* by Robert V. Bruce

1989. (two winners) *Battle Cry of Freedom: The Civil War Era* by James M. McPherson and *Parting the Waters: America in theKing Years 1954-1963* by Taylor Branch

1990. *In Our Image: America's Empire in the Philippines* by Stanley Karnow

1991. *A Midwife's Tale* by Laurel Thatcher Ulrich

1992. *The Fate of Liberty: Abraham Lincoln and Civil Liberties* by Mark E. Neely Jr.

1993. *The Radicalism of the American Revolution* by Gordon S. Wood

1994. No award given.

1995. *No Ordinary Time: Franklin and Eleanor Roosevelt: The Home Front in World War II* by Doris Kearns Goodwin

1996. *William Cooper's Town: Power and Persuasion on the Frontier of the Early American Republic* by Alan Taylor

1997. *Original Meanings: Politics and Ideas in the Making of the Constitution* by Jack N. Rakove

1998. *Summer for the Gods: The Scopes Trial and America's Continuing Debate Over Science and Religion* by Edward J. Larson

1999. *Gotham: A History of New York City to 1898* by Edwin G. Burrows and Mike Wallace

2000. *Freedom from Fear: The American People in Depression and War, 1929-1945* by David M. Kennedy

2001. *Founding Brothers: The Revolutionary Generation* by Joseph J. Ellis

2002. *The Metaphysical Club: A Story of Ideas in America* by Louis Menand

2003. *An Army at Dawn: The War in North Africa 1942–1943*
by Rick Atkinson
2004. *A Nation Under Our Feet* by Steven Hahn
2005. *Washington's Crossing* by David Hackett Fischer
2006. *Polio: An American Story* by David Oshinsky
2007. *The Race Beat* by Gene Roberts and Hank Klibanoff
2008. *What Hath God Wrought: the Transformation of America, 1815–1848* by Daniel Walker Howe
2009. *The Hemingses of Monticello: An American Family*
by Annette Gordon-Reed
2010. *Lords of Finance: The Bankers Who Broke the World*
by Liaquat Ahamed
2011. *The Fiery Trial: Abraham Lincoln and American Slavery*
by Eric Foner
2012. *Malcolm X: A Life of Reinvention* by Manning Marable
2013. *Embers of War: The Fall of an Empire and the Making of America's Vietnam* by Fredrik Logevall
2014. *The Internal Enemy: Slavery and War in Virginia, 1772–1832* by Alan Taylor

~~~~~~~~~~~~

THE PULITZER PRIZE FOR BIOGRAPHY OR AUTOBIOGRAPHY

1980. *The Rise of Theodore Roosevelt* by Edmund Morris
1981. *Peter the Great: His Life and World* by Robert K. Massie
1982. *Grant: A Biography* by William S. McFeely
1983. *Growing Up* by Russell Baker
1984. *Booker T. Washington: The Wizard of Tuskegee, 1901–1915* by Louis R. Harlan
1985. *The Life and Times of Cotton Mather* by Kenneth Silverman
1986. *Louise Bogan: A Portrait* by Elizabeth Frank
1987. *Bearing the Cross: Martin Luther King Jr. and the Southern Christian Leadership Conference* by David J. Garrow

2011. *Washington: A Life* by Ron Chernow

2012. *George F. Kennan: An American Life* by John Lewis Gaddis

2013. *The Black Count: Glory, Revolution, Betrayal, and the Real Count of Monte Cristo* by Tom Reiss

2014. *Margaret Fuller: A New American Life* by Megan Marshall

THE PULITZER PRIZE FOR POETRY

1980. *Selected Poems* by Donald Justice

1981. *The Morning of the Poem* by James Schuyler

1982. *The Collected Poems* by Sylvia Plath

1983. *Selected Poems* by Galway Kinnell

1984. *American Primitive* by Mary Oliver

1985. *Yin* by Carolyn Kizer

1986. *The Flying Change* by Henry S. Taylor

1987. *Thomas and Beulah* by Rita Dove

1988. *Partial Accounts: New and Selected Poems* by William Meredith

1989. *New and Collected Poems* by Richard Wilbur

1990. *The World Doesn't End* by Charles Simic

1991. *Near Changes* by Mona Van Duyn

1992. *Selected Poems* by James Tate

1993. *The Wild Iris* by Louise Glück

1994. *Neon Vernacular: New and Selected Poems* by Yusef Komunyakaa

1995. *The Simple Truth* by Philip Levine

1996. *The Dream of the Unified Field* by Jorie Graham

1997. *Alive Together: New and Selected Poems* by Lisel Mueller

1998. *Black Zodiac* by Charles Wright

1999. *Blizzard of One* by Mark Strand

2000. *Repair* by C. K. Williams

2001. *Different Hours* by Stephen Dunn

2002. *Practical Gods* by Carl Dennis

2003. *Moy Sand and Gravel* by Paul Muldoon

2004. *Walking to Martha's Vineyard* by Franz Wright

2005. *Delights & Shadows* by Ted Kooser

2006. *Late Wife* by Claudia Emerson

2007. *Native Guard* by Natasha Trethewey

2008. (two winners) *Time and Materials* by Robert Hass
      and *Failure* by Philip Schultz

2009. *The Shadow of Sirius* by W. S. Merwin

2010. *Versed* by Rae Armantrout

2011. *The Best of It: New and Selected Poems* by Kay Ryan

2012. *Life on Mars* by Tracy K. Smith

2013. *Stag's Leap* by Sharon Olds

2014. *3 Sections* by Vijay Seshadri

THE MAN BOOKER PRIZE

1980. *The Beggar Maid* by Alice Munroe

1981. *Midnight's Children* by Salman Rushdie

1982. *Schindler's Ark* by Thomas Keneally

1983. *Life & Times of Michael K* by J. M. Coetzee

1984. *Hotel du Luc* by Anita Brookner

1985. *The Bone People* by Keri Hulme

1986. *The Old Devil* by Kingsley Amis

1987. *Moon Tiger* by Penelope Lively

1988. *Oscar and Lucinda* by Peter Carey

1989. *The Remains of the Day* by Kazuo Ishiguro

1990. *Possession: A Romance* by A. S. Byatt

1991. *The Famished Road* by Ben Okra

1992. *The English Patient* by Michael Ondaatje

1993. *Paddy Clarke Ha Ha Ha* by Roddy Doyle

1994. *How Late It Was, How Late* by James Kelman

1995. *The Ghost Road* by Pat Barker

1996. *Last Orders* by Graham Swift

1997. *The God of Small Things* by Arundhati Roy

1998. *Amsterdam* by Ian McEwan

1999. *Disgrace* by J. M. Coetzee

2000. *The Blind Assassin* by Margaret Atwood

2001. *True History of the Kelly Gang* by Peter Carey

2002. *Life of Pi* by Yann Martel

2003. *Vernon God Little* by DBC Pierre

2004. *The Line of Beauty* by Alan Hollinghurst

2005. *The Sea* by Jon Banville

2006. *The Inheritance of Loss* by Kiran Desai

2007. *The Gathering* by Ann Enright

2008. *The White Tiger* by Aravind Adiga

2009. *Wolf Hall* by Hilary Mantel

2010. *The Finkler Question* by Howard Jacobson

2011. *The Sense of an Ending* by Julian Barnes

2012. *Bring Up the Bodies* by Hilary Mantel

2013. *The Luminaries* by Eleanor Catton

THE NOBEL PRIZE IN LITERATURE

1980. Czeslaw Milosz, Poland and the United States

1981. Elias Canetti, United Kingdom

1982. Gabriel García Márquez, Colombia

1983. William Golding, United Kingdom

1984. Jaroslav Seifert, Czechoslovakia

1985. Claude Simon, France

1986. Wole Soyinka, Nigeria

1987. Joseph Brodsky, United States

1988. Naguib Mahfouz, Egypt

1989. Camilo José Cela, Spain

1990. Octavio Paz, Mexico

1991. Nadine Gordimer, South Africa

1992. Derek Walcott, Saint Lucia
1993. Toni Morrison, United States
1994. Kenzaburo Oe, Japan
1995. Seamus Heaney, Ireland
1996. Wislawa Szymborska, Poland
1997. Dario Fo, Italy
1998. José Saramago, Portugal
1999. Günter Grass, Germany
2000. Gao Xingjian, France
2001. V. S. Naipaul, United Kingdom
2002. Imre Kertész, Hungary
2003. J. M. Coetzee, South Africa
2004. Elfriede Jelinek, Austria
2005. Harold Pinter, United Kingdom
2006. Orhan Pamuk, Turkey
2007. Doris Lessing, United Kingdom
2008. Jean-Marie Gustave Le Clézio, France and Mauritius
2009. Herta Müller, Romania and Germany
2010. Mario Vargas Llosa, Peru
2011. Tomas Tranströmer, Sweden
2012. Mo Yan, China
2013. Alice Munro, Canada

THE NEW YORK PUBLIC LIBRARY
MOST BORROWED BOOKS

Fiction

Inferno by Dan Brown
And the Mountains Echoed by Khaled Hosseini
Revenge Wears Prada by Lauren Weisberger
The Casual Vacancy by J. K. Rowling
Gone Girl by Gillian Flynn

The Walking Dead by Robert Kirkman
First Sight by Danielle Steel
W is for Wasted by Sue Grafton
Never Go Back by Lee Child

Nonfiction

Lean In: Women, Work, and the Will to Lead by Sheryl Sandberg
Let's Explore Diabetes with Owls by David Sedaris
My Beloved World by Sonia Sotomayor
VB6: Eat Vegan Before 6:00 to Lose Weight and Restore Your Health . . . for Good by Mark Bittman
Salt, Sugar, Fat: How the Food Giants Hooked Us by Michael Moss
Cooked: A Natural History of Transformation by Michael Pollan
Crack the GED by Geoff Martz
Dad Is Fat by Jim Gaffigan
The Examined Life: How We Love and Find Ourselves by Stephen Grosz
Thinking, Fast and Slow by Daniel Kahneman

~~~~~~~~~~~~~~~~~

OPRAH'S BOOK CLUB

1996

The Deep End of the Ocean by Jacquelyn Mitchard
Song of Solomon by Toni Morrison
The Book of Ruth by Jane Hamilton
She's Come Undone by Wally Lamb

1997

Stones from the River by Ursula Hegi
The Rapture of Canaan by Sheri Reynolds
The Heart of a Woman by Maya Angelou
Songs in Ordinary Time by Mary McGarry Morris
The Meanest Thing to Say by Bill Cosby

A Lesson Before Dying by Ernest J. Gaines
A Virtuous Woman by Kaye Gibbons
Ellen Foster by Kaye Gibbons
The Treasure Hunt by Bill Cosby
The Best Way to Play by Bill Cosby

1998

Paradise by Toni Morrison
Here on Earth by Alice Hoffman
Black and Blue by Anna Quindlen
Breath, Eyes, Memory by Edwidge Danticat
I Know This Much Is True by Wally Lamb
What Looks Like Crazy on an Ordinary Day by Pearl Cleage
Midwives by Chris Bohjalian
Where the Heart Is by Billie Letts

1999

Jewel by Bret Lott
The Reader by Bernhard Schlink
The Pilot's Wife by Anita Shreve
White Oleander by Janet Fitch
Mother of Pearl by Melinda Haynes
Tara Road by Maeve Binchy
River, Cross My Heart by Breena Clarke
Vinegar Hill by A. Manette Ansay
A Map of the World by Jane Hamilton

2000

Gap Creek by Robert Morgan
Daughter of Fortune by Isabel Allende
Back Roads by Tawni O'Dell
The Bluest Eye by Toni Morrison
While I Was Gone by Sue Miller
The Poisonwood Bible by Barbara Kingsolver
Open House by Elizabeth Berg
Drowning Ruth by Christina Schwarz
House of Sand and Fog by Andre Dubus III

2001

We Were the Mulvaneys by Joyce Carol Oates

Icy Sparks by Gwyn Hyman Rubio

Stolen Lives: Twenty Years in a Desert Jail by Malika Oufkir

Cane River by Lalita Tademy

The Corrections by Jonathan Franzen

A Fine Balance by Rohinton Mistry

2002

Fall on Your Knees by Ann-Marie MacDonald

Sula by Toni Morrison

2003

East of Eden by John Steinbeck

Cry, the Beloved Country by Alan Paton

2004

One Hundred Years of Solitude by Gabriel García Márquez

The Heart Is a Lonely Hunter by Carson McCullers

Anna Karenina by Leo Tolstoy

The Good Earth by Pearl S. Buck

2005

The Sound and the Fury; As I Lay Dying; Light in August
    by William Faulkner

A Million Little Pieces by James Frey

2006

Night by Elie Wiesel

2007

The Measure of a Man: A Spiritual Autobiography
    by Sir Sidney Poitier

The Road by Cormac McCarthy

Middlesex by Jeffrey Eugenides

Love in the Time of Cholera by Gabriel García Márquez

The Pillars of the Earth by Ken Follett

2008

A New Earth by Eckhart Tolle

The Story of Edgar Sawtelle by David Wroblewski

2009

Say You're One of Them by Uwem Akpan

2010

Freedom by Jonathan Franzen

Great Expectations; A Tale of Two Cities by Charles Dickens

OPRAH'S BOOK CLUB 2.0

2012

Wild: From Lost to Found on the Pacific Crest Trail
    by Cheryl Strayed

The Twelve Tribes of Hattie by Ayan Matthis

2014

The Invention of Wings by Sue Monk Kidd

A NOTE BY THE COMPILER

If I were a determined determinist, I would imagine that I was destined to preside over a journal about reading. During my childhood, polio, bronchitis, scarlet fever, and other maladies made me an invalid incapable of being the centerfielder I wanted to be. I responded by turning my sickroom into a library. Besides perusing my latest finds, my greatest joys were my foraging adventures with my father to the Fourth Avenue shops of Manhattan's "used bookstore row" and our rhapsodic afternoons at the New York Public Library. My first job, quite logically, was in the Westfield Public Library. In college, I renewed my obsession, skipping meals to buy books. Since then, I have spent decades working in two bookstores, helping customers, running a book information service, and purchasing private libraries; writing and editing magazines about books; and writing, editing, and publishing books myself. I cannot imagine a day without reading and, yet with all these words, I have never been able to adequately express the pleasures it has given me.